Greetings
California!

·HSP·
CALIFORNIA
EXCURSIONS

It takes you there!

HSP CALIFORNIA EXCURSIONS

Make a Splash

Senior Authors

Isabel L. Beck • Roger C. Farr • Dorothy S. Strickland

Authors

Alma Flor Ada • Roxanne F. Hudson • Margaret G. McKeown

Robin C. Scarcella • Julie A. Washington

Harcourt

SCHOOL PUBLISHERS

www.harcourtschool.com

HSP CALIFORNIA EXCURSIONS

Make a Splash

Harcourt

SCHOOL PUBLISHERS

www.harcourtschool.com

Theme 3
Turning Corners

Contents

Lesson 7

Decodable Story

Theme Writing

Student Writing Model: Describing an Event

Social Studies

Social Studies

Paired Selections

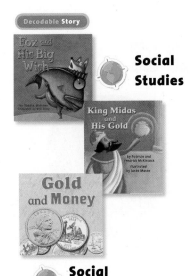

Lesson 12

Theme Big Books

"The Frog and the Ox"

Decodable Books 7–12

Comprehension Strategies

Before You Read

Look at the pictures. Think about what you already know.

Set a purpose.

I want to find out about frogs.

While You Read

Ask questions.

What do frogs eat?

Reread.

I'll read this page again.

Answer questions.

Oh! Some frogs eat bugs.

After You Read

Summarize.

First, tadpoles hatch from eggs. Then, they begin changing into frogs. Last, they are full-grown frogs.

Make connections.

This is like another book I read. I learned about how butterflies change.

READING-WRITING
CONNECTION

CALIFORNIA STANDARDS
ENGLISH-LANGUAGE ARTS
STANDARDS

Reading 1.10 Generate
the sounds from all the
letters and letter patterns,
including consonant blends
and long- and short-vowel
patterns (i.e., phonograms),
and blend those sounds into
recognizable words.

Reading 3.1 Identify and
describe the elements
of plot, setting, and
character(s) in a story,
as well as the story's
beginning, middle, and
ending.

Theme **3** Turning Corners

The Gardeners, Judy Byford

13

Contents

Lesson 7

1 Decodable Story

Ten Eggs

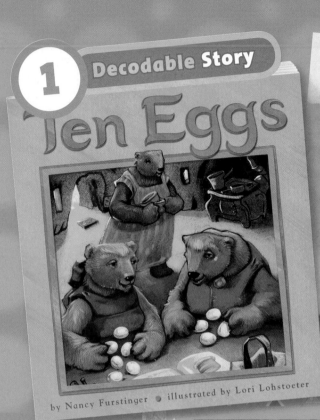

by Nancy Furstinger ● illustrated by Lori Lohstoeter

2 Genre: Fantasy

Little Red Hen
Gets Help

by Kenneth Spengler
illustrated by Margaret Spengler

Let's Make
Tortillas!

3 Genre: Recipe

Ten Eggs

Ten Eggs

by Nancy Furstinger

illustrated
by Lori Lohstoeter

Ten hens had ten eggs.

Jen got six eggs.
Ken got the rest.

Jen mixed the eggs.
Ken mixed the eggs.

What a big mess!

Did Jen and Ken get help?

Yes! Mom got a pan.
In went the eggs.

What did Mom make?
The best eggs yet!

Phonics Skill

Short Vowel <u>e</u>

The letter <u>e</u> can stand for the sound at the beginning of the words **<u>egg</u>** and **<u>elephant</u>**.

egg   **elephant**

The letter <u>e</u> can stand for the sound in the middle of the words **p<u>e</u>n** and **n<u>e</u>t**.

pen   **net**

CALIFORNIA STANDARDS
ENGLISH-LANGUAGE ARTS STANDARDS—Reading 1.10 Generate the sounds from all the letters and letter patterns, including consonant blends and long- and short-vowel patterns (i.e., phonograms), and blend those sounds into recognizable words.

Look at each picture. Read the words.
Tell which word names the picture.

ten

hen

him

vent

vat

vest

 www.harcourtschool.com/reading

Try This!

Read the sentences.

I have a pet.

He is called Jet.

He went to the vet.

Now he can rest.

25

Words to Know

High-Frequency Words

R1.11

day

said

eat

first

time

was

CALIFORNIA STANDARDS
ENGLISH-LANGUAGE ARTS STANDARDS—Reading 1.11 Read common, irregular sight words (e.g., *the, have, said, come, give, of*).

26

"It is a hot **day**," **said** Hen.

"Let's **eat**," said Cat.

"**First** add some of this," said Fox.

"Now it is **time** to add this," said Pig.

"That **was** fast!" said Hen.

GO online www.harcourtschool.com/reading

Little Red Hen Gets Help

by Kenneth Spengler
Illustrated by Margaret Spengler

Fantasy

Award Winner

Genre Study

A **fantasy** is a made-up story. The events could never really happen.

What Little Red Hen Asks	What the Characters Say and Do

R2.2

Comprehension Strategy

Answer Questions To answer questions about the story, think about the words you read. Use what you already know to figure out answers, too.

CALIFORNIA STANDARDS
ENGLISH-LANGUAGE ARTS STANDARDS—Reading 2.2
Respond to *who, what, when, where,* and *how* questions.

Little Red Hen Gets Help

by Kenneth Spengler

illustrated by Margaret Spengler

One day, Little Red Hen got up.
She was hungry.

"Who wants to eat this?" she asked.

"Not I," said Cat.

"I can't," said Fox.

"Oh, no," said Pig.

"Who wants tacos?" asked Red Hen.

"I do!" they all yelled.

"Will you help make some tacos?"

"Yes!" said Cat.

"I will!" said Fox.

"Let me, too!" said Pig.

Red Hen fed Cat, Fox, and Pig.

"What a mess! Who will pick up?"

"Not I," said Cat.

"I can't," said Fox.

"Oh, no," said Pig.

"We will help!" called the ants.

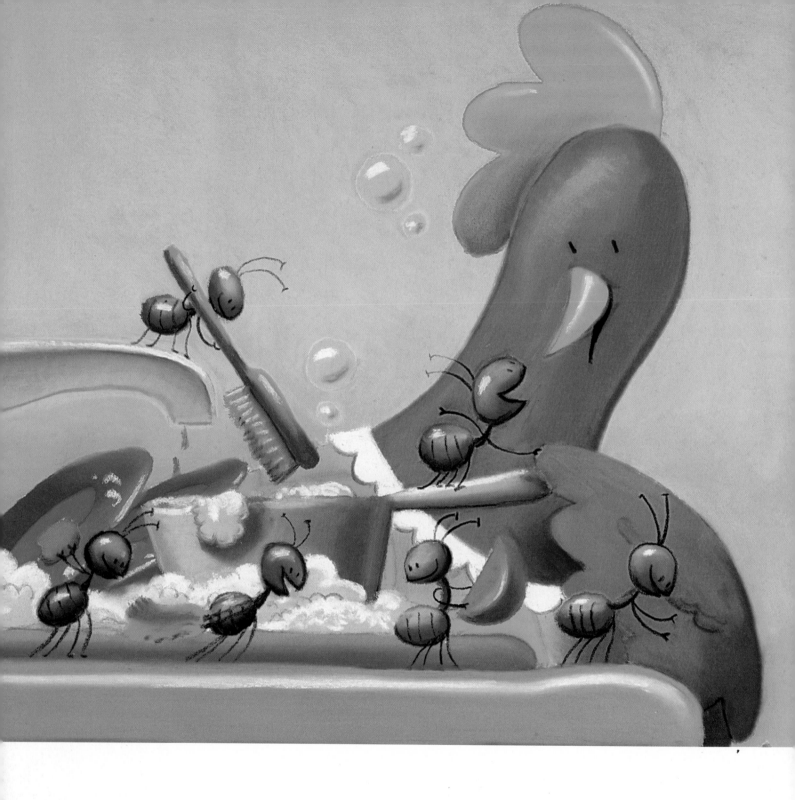

"Thank you, ants" said Red Hen.
"Next time, I will ask you first!"

Think Critically

R2.2
R2.7
R3.1
W2.1

1 How are the ants like Cat, Pig, and Fox? How are they different?

COMPARE AND CONTRAST

2 What happens to the kitchen when Cat, Pig, and Fox make tacos? DETAILS

3 Why does Little Red Hen need help cleaning? MAKE INFERENCES

4 Why does Little Red Hen say she will ask the ants first to help her next time? DRAW CONCLUSIONS

5 **WRITE** Write about a time when someone helped you. WRITING RESPONSE

CALIFORNIA STANDARDS
ENGLISH-LANGUAGE ARTS STANDARDS—Reading 2.2 Respond to *who, what, when, where,* and *how* questions; **Reading 2.7** Retell the central ideas of simple expository or narrative passages; **Reading 3.1** Identify and describe the elements of plot, setting, and character(s) in a story, as well as the story's beginning, middle, and ending; **Writing 2.1** Write brief narratives (e.g., fictional, autobiographical) describing an experience.

Meet the Author
Kenneth Spengler

Kenneth Spengler likes to write funny stories.
He worked with his wife, Margaret, on this one.

"I liked writing this story because I love food,
especially tacos! Just like the Little Red Hen, I like
help when I cook. Sometimes we spill food on the
floor. Our dog, Jackie, helps clean it up, though,
not ants!"

Meet the Illustrator
Margaret Spengler

Margaret Spengler is the artist who made the pictures for this story. She painted them on sand paper with pastel chalk and water. The thing she likes best about being an artist is being creative.

"I like the Little Red Hen because she is smart and caring. I also like the way she shares with her friends.**"**

Let's Make Tortillas!

Recipe

Let's Make Tortillas!

1½ cups flour

½ teaspoon salt

2 tablespoons oil

½ cup warm water

 **1** Mix the flour, salt, oil, and water.

2 Roll six balls.
Make six circles.

3 Cook in a pan.

4 Eat the tortillas!
You can fill them
to make tacos.

Connections

Comparing Texts

R2.2
R2.6
R3.3

1 What did you find out about making tacos from the story? What did you learn from the recipe?

2 How do you help clean up at home?

3 Which of Little Red Hen's jobs would you do best? Tell why.

Writing W2.1

Imagine that you are in the story. Write about how you would help.

What Little Red Hen Asks	How I Would Help

Make and read new words.

Start with **egg**.

Add **l** in front of **e**. Take off **g**.

Change **g** to **t**.

Change **l** to **w**.

Add **n** after **e**.

Fluency Practice

Work with a small group. Decide who will be each animal in "Little Red Hen Gets Help." Read the story. Use your voice to show how your character feels. Look at the end marks of sentences to help you.

I will!

Yes!

Let me, too!

Reading 2.2 Respond to *who, what, when, where,* and *how* questions; **Reading 2.6** Relate prior knowledge to textual information; **Reading 3.3** Recollect, talk, and write about books read during the school year; **Writing 2.1** Write brief narratives (e.g., fictional, autobiographical) describing an experience; **Written and Oral English Language Conventions 1.4** Distinguish between declarative, exclamatory, and interrogative sentences.

Reading-Writing Connection

Describing an Event

"Little Red Hen Gets Help" is about something that Little Red Hen and her friends did. After we read the story, we wrote about something that we did.

▶ **First, we talked about the story.**

▶ **Next, we talked about things we have done. We made up sentences to tell about an event.**

▶ **Last, we read our sentences.**

Our class went to the zoo. We saw lions, bears, and many other animals. We ate lunch at the zoo, and then we came home. We all had a great time!

Contents

Lesson 8

Thanks, Seth!

by Anne Mansk
illustrated by Linda Bronson

Ben is not glad.
"Can I do this math?"

Seth sees Ben.
"I can help Ben," thinks Seth.

Ben sees Seth.
Seth tells Ben he can help.

Seth helps Ben with the task.

Now Ben can add fast.

Seth and Ben are glad!
Ben did all the math.

Thanks, Seth!

Focus Skill

 **Details**

Details give small bits of information about something. Details help you picture the person, animal, place, or thing in your mind.

MILK

Look at the picture.

It shows details of what this child is having for lunch.

Tell about this picture. What details do you see?

 Try This!

Look at the picture. Tell how the details help you understand what is happening.

Words to Know

don't

says

water

Mr.

new

line

her

CALIFORNIA STANDARDS
ENGLISH-LANGUAGE ARTS STANDARDS—Reading 1.11 Read common, irregular sight words (e.g., *the, have, said, come, give, of*).

"I **don't** have a job," **says** Beth.

"You can **water** this plant," **Mr.** Hall says.

Max has a **new** job, too.

He helps Hops.

We get in **line** to pet **her**.

GO online www.harcourtschool.com/reading

Beth's Job

by Carole Roberts
illustrated by Michael Garland

Realistic Fiction

Genre Study

Realistic fiction stories are made up, but they could happen in real life.

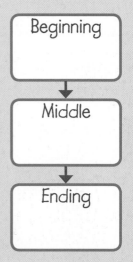

Beginning

↓

Middle

↓

Ending

R3.1

Comprehension Strategy

Use Graphic Organizers

A story map can help you understand and remember the beginning, middle, and ending of a story.

CALIFORNIA STANDARDS
ENGLISH-LANGUAGE ARTS STANDARDS—
Reading 3.1 Identify and describe the elements of plot, setting, and character(s) in a story, as well as the story's beginning, middle, and ending.

Beth's Job

by Carole Roberts

illustrated by Michael Garland

It's the day for new jobs.

Class Jobs
Max - pet
Beth - plant
Ann - eggs
Jeff - line
Glen - flag
Jill - clock

Monday

"What is my job?" asks Beth.

"You can water the plant,"
says Mr. Hall.

Class Jobs
Max - pet
Beth - plant
Ann - eggs
Jeff - line
Glen - flag
Jill - c

Monday

"Oh, no," thinks Beth.

Max helps with Hops.
Hops is the class pet.

"I want that job," thinks Beth.

Ann helps with the eggs.

Beth wants that job.

Jeff is first in line.

Beth wants that job, too.

Glen gets to hold the flag.

"I want to hold the flag,"
thinks Beth.

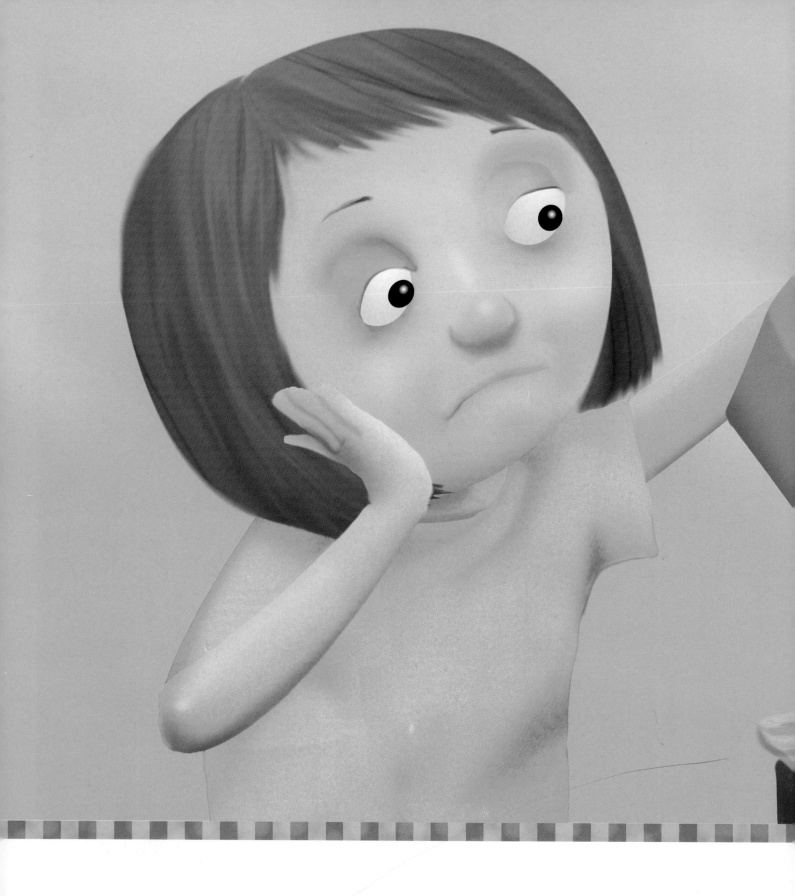

"I don't like this plant," thinks Beth.

"I want a new job."

"Look at this flower, Beth!"
says Mr. Hall.

"Oh, my!" says the class.

"Oh, my!" says Beth.
"How did that get there?"

"This job is the best!"
Beth likes her job at last!

Think Critically

R2.2
R2.7
W2.1

1 How does Beth feel about her job when the story begins? How does she feel at the end? Why?

COMPARE AND CONTRAST

2 What is one thing Beth does to help the plant? DETAILS

3 Why do you think Beth wants to help with the eggs? MAKE INFERENCES

4 How does Beth's job make the classroom a better place?

DRAW CONCLUSIONS

5 **WRITE** Write about a job you enjoy doing. Tell why that job is important. WRITING RESPONSE

CALIFORNIA STANDARDS
ENGLISH-LANGUAGE ARTS STANDARDS—Reading 2.2 Respond to *who, what, when, where,* and *how* questions; **Reading 2.7** Retell the central ideas of simple expository or narrative passages; **Writing 2.1** Write brief narratives (e.g., fictional, autobiographical) describing an experience.

Meet the Illustrator
Michael Garland

Michael Garland has written and illustrated many books for children. He spent his childhood in New York exploring the woods, playing sports, and drawing. Drawing was the thing he did best. When he would draw something in school, his teachers would often show it to the class and put it up on the bulletin board. This helped him to decide he wanted to become an artist.

GO online www.harcourtschool.com/reading

Flowers Grow

Nonfiction

Flowers Grow

A plant needs water, light, air, and soil to grow.

seed

seedling

young plant

bud

flower

The plant grows.

Now there is a flower.
How nice!

Contents

Lesson 9

1 Decodable **Story**

A Nut Falls
by Sandra Widener
illustrated by Doug Bowles

2 Genre: Nonfiction

Plants Can't Jump
by Ned Crowley

3 Genre: Poetry

Cornfield Leaves
by Lessie Jones Little
illustrated by Don Tate

Phonics
Words with short vowel <u>u</u>

Words to Know

Review

now

tree

A Nut Falls

by Sandra Widener
illustrated by
Doug Bowles

Thud! A nut falls in mud.

Sun falls on that nut.
Next that nut gets wet.

The stem pops up!
That nut is now a small plant.

The plant is tall.
It is a big nut tree!

Small buds are on that tree.
Small nuts are on that tree.

Small nuts get big.
Men pick nuts off the tree.

A nut fell in mud.
That nut is now a big tree!

Focus Skill

 # Details

Details give small bits of information about something. Details can tell what something looks like, how it sounds, or what it does.

Look at the picture.

The artist is drawing details he sees in the real flower.

Tell about this picture. What details do you see?

Look closely at the picture. Think about the details you see. Tell what you think this machine does.

Words to Know

High-Frequency Words

R1.11

live

does

grow

many

be

food

CALIFORNIA STANDARDS
ENGLISH-LANGUAGE ARTS STANDARDS—Reading 1.11 Read common, irregular sight words (e.g., *the, have, said, come, give, of*).

Where can a plant **live**?

Where **does** it **grow**?

Many plants can **be food**.

Many can grow flowers.

Nonfiction

Genre Study

A **nonfiction** selection tells about things that are real and often has photographs.

K	W	L
What I Know	What I Want to Know	What I Learned

Comprehension Strategy

Monitor Comprehension: Reading Rate Read along smoothly with the rhythm and rhyme of this nonfiction poem. Slow down to read important information.

Plants Can't Jump

by Ned Crowley

Plants can't jump!
Plants can't hop.

Just add water,
and up they pop!

Roots grow down.
Stems grow up.

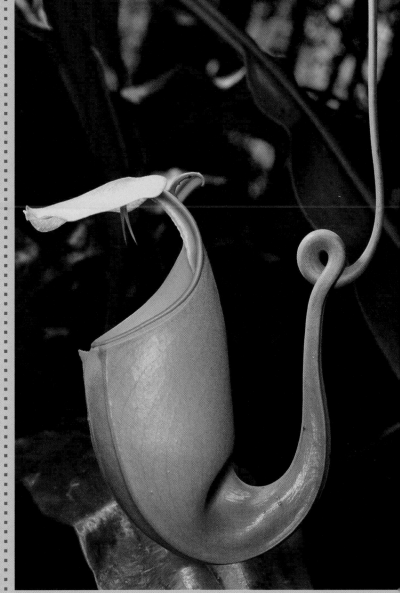

Plants can look like
bells and cups.

Plants have spots
and dots and bumps.

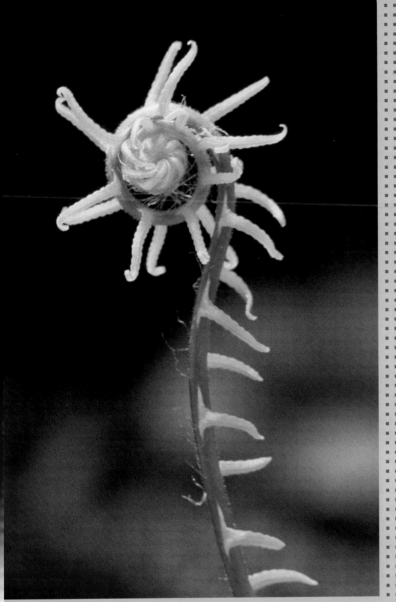

Plants can be thin.
Plants can be plump.

A plant has leaves,
but what do they give?

Leaves make food
so a plant can live.

Plants must get water.
It helps them grow.

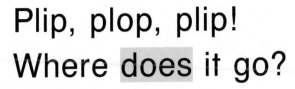

Plip, plop, plip!
Where does it go?

Plants live in sand.
Plants live in mud.

This plant has flowers.
That one has a bud.

If some bugs want food,
they eat plants.

Some plants eat bugs
like moths and ants!

Plants are red
and pink and black.

Many plants are food,
so grab a snack!

Plants can't jump,
but they don't fuss.

Plants can grow,
just like us!

125

Think Critically

R2.2
R2.7
W2.2

1 What do leaves do for plants?

DRAW CONCLUSIONS

2 What do a plant's roots do? What does the stem do? DETAILS

3 What are different ways a plant can get water? DRAW CONCLUSIONS

4 Why do you think some plants eat bugs? MAKE INFERENCES

5 **WRITE** Which do you like better— a plant with flowers or a plant you can eat? Tell why. WRITING RESPONSE

CALIFORNIA STANDARDS
ENGLISH-LANGUAGE ARTS STANDARDS—Reading 2.2 Respond to *who, what, when, where,* and *how* questions; **Reading 2.7** Retell the central ideas of simple expository or narrative passages; **Writing 2.2** Write brief expository descriptions of a real object, person, place, or event, using sensory details.

Meet the Author
Ned Crowley

Ned Crowley is a writer and illustrator. Recently, he has been writing books about bugs and plants. Mr. Crowley says books like these are fun to write. When he looks at pictures of plants or bugs, he tries to give them personalities just like people.

Mr. Crowley has three daughters. He says that they like plants a lot more than bugs!

 www.harcourtschool.com/reading

Teacher Read-Aloud

Cornfield Leaves

by Lessie Jones Little
Illustrated by Don Tate

Poetry

Cornfield Leaves

by Lessie Jones Little
illustrated by Don Tate

Silky ribbons long and green,
Dotted with sparkling dew,
Waving in the summer breeze
Under a roof of blue.

Keep on waving in the breeze,
Keep on sparkling, too,
And every time you wave at me,
I'll wave right back at you.

Contents

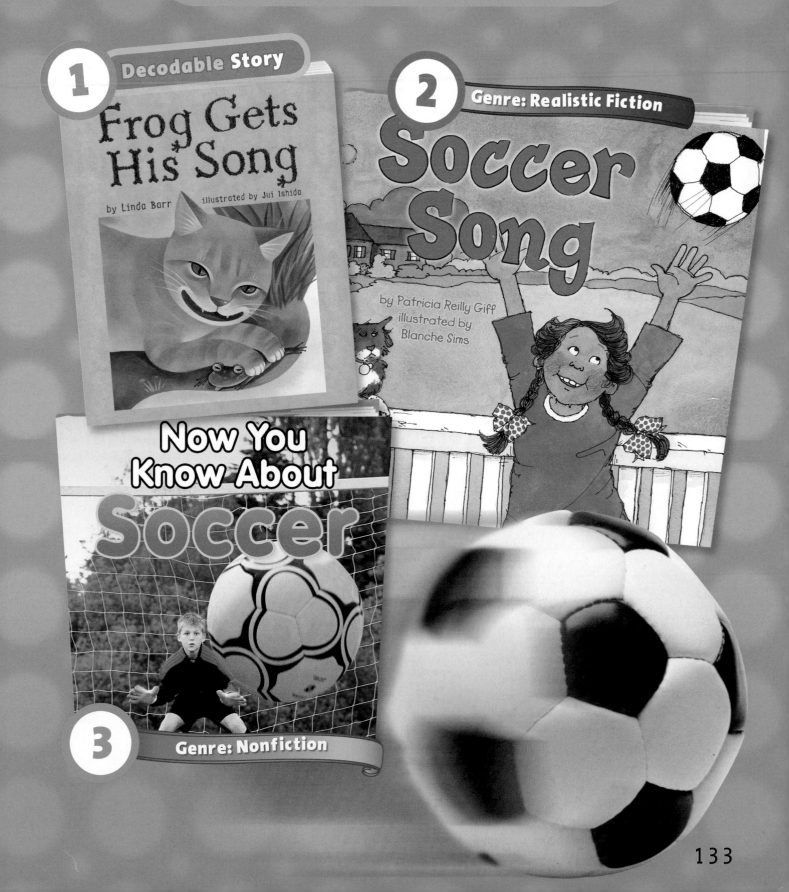

1 Decodable Story

Frog Gets His Song

by Linda Barr   illustrated by Jui Ishida

2 Genre: Realistic Fiction

Soccer Song

by Patricia Reilly Giff
illustrated by
Blanche Sims

Now You Know About

Soccer

3 Genre: Nonfiction

Frog Gets His Song

by Linda Barr

illustrated by Jui Ishida

Ming had Frog in her grip.
Ming looked at him with a big grin.

Frog looked at Ming's long
fangs. "Help!" yelled Frog.
"Let me go!"

"Be still!" Ming hissed. "Sing me a song and I will let you go."

"Sing?" grunted Frog. "Frogs can't sing!"

"Do frogs have lungs?" Ming asked.

"Yes," Frog said.

"Then sing!" Ming snapped.

Frog filled his lungs and sang.
His song rang out. Frog sang
and sang and sang.

Did Ming let Frog go? Yes.
Did Frog stop singing? No!

Frogs are still singing!

Focus Skill

Plot

The events that make up a story are called the **plot**. The **plot** of a story is what happens in that story.

Look at the pictures.

These pictures show a story. The plot is about children finding a lost dog.

CALIFORNIA STANDARDS
ENGLISH-LANGUAGE ARTS STANDARDS—Reading 3.1 Identify and describe the elements of plot, setting, and character(s) in a story, as well as the story's beginning, middle, and ending.

The pictures show events in a story.
What is the plot?

Try This!

Look at the picture. Choose the words that name the plot of a story about these people.

- enjoying winter activities

- playing with pets

- having a picnic

 www.harcourtschool.com/reading

Words to Know

High-Frequency Words

R1.11

school

every

your

feet

use

arms

head

way

CALIFORNIA STANDARDS
ENGLISH-LANGUAGE ARTS STANDARDS—Reading 1.11 Read common, irregular sight words (e.g., *the, have, said, come, give, of*).

You can have fun at **school every** day.

Run and jump with **your feet**.

Use your feet to kick the ball.

Use your **arms** and **head**, too.

You can block the ball this **way**.

145

Soccer Song

by Patricia Reilly Giff
Illustrated by Blanche Sims

Realistic Fiction

Award-Winning Author and Illustrator

R3.1

Genre Study

Realistic fiction stories have a beginning, middle, and ending. Characters do things that could happen in real life.

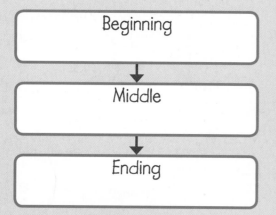

Beginning

↓

Middle

↓

Ending

R3.1

Comprehension Strategy

Recognize Story Structure As you read, think about what is happening in each part of the story.

CALIFORNIA STANDARDS
ENGLISH-LANGUAGE ARTS STANDARDS—
Reading 3.1 Identify and describe the elements of plot, setting, and character(s) in a story, as well as the story's beginning, middle, and ending.

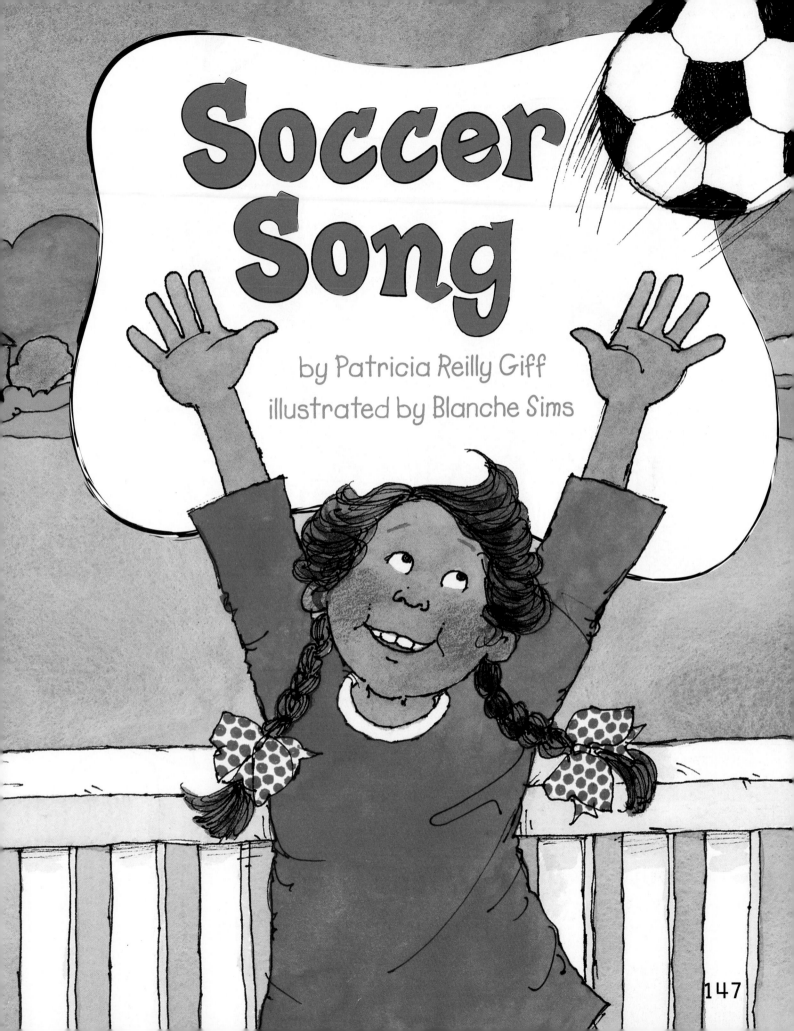

Soccer Song

by Patricia Reilly Giff

illustrated by Blanche Sims

Jill had long arms.
She had strong hands.

One day, Jill got Gus.
"Jill did it!" called Tom.
"Meow," said Gus.

One day, Fran swung the bat.
Her ball went up.
Jill jumped up.

"Jill got it!" yelled the kids.
"Meow," said Gus.

At school, Miss King said,
"It's soccer time! Kick the
ball with your feet."

"Don't use your hands!"
said Tom.

Jill's legs went this way.
The ball went that way.

Jill's head went this way.
The ball went that way.

Jill hung her head.

"You have strong arms and hands," said Tom. "You got Gus out of a tree."

"You got my ball, too," said Fran.

"A goalie can use her hands," said Miss King.

158

The next day, Jill was goalie. She
used her strong arms and hands.
She blocked the ball every time.

"You did it!" yelled Tom and Fran.

"Jump, block! I am strong!
This is my soccer song!" sang Jill.
"Meow!" sang Gus.

Think Critically

R2.2
R2.6
R2.7
W2.2

1 Why does Jill have trouble learning to play soccer at first? PLOT

2 What are some things that Jill can do well? DETAILS

3 Why is Jill a good goalie? DRAW CONCLUSIONS

4 Do you think Jill will keep playing soccer? Tell why or why not. MAKE INFERENCES

5 **WRITE** Write about something you can do well. WRITING RESPONSE

CALIFORNIA STANDARDS
ENGLISH-LANGUAGE ARTS STANDARDS—Reading 2.2 Respond to *who, what, when, where,* and *how* questions; **Reading 2.6** Relate prior knowledge to textual information; **Reading 2.7** Retell the central ideas of simple expository or narrative passages; **Writing 2.2** Write brief expository descriptions of a real object, person, place, or event, using sensory details.

Meet the Author
Patricia Reilly Giff

Patricia Reilly Giff has written many books. In her stories, children do some of the same things you do!

"I enjoyed writing this story because my grandchildren love soccer. My new granddaughter's name is Jillian. We call her Jill, just like the character in my story."

Meet the Illustrator
Blanche Sims

Blanche Sims has illustrated many children's books. She says that the best part about being an artist is drawing. She has always loved to draw! When Blanche Sims was in school, one of her teachers even hung up a huge piece of paper in the classroom for her to fill with her artwork.

Meow

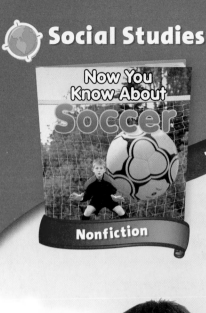

Now You Know About
Soccer

Nonfiction

Now You Know About
Soccer

People all over the world play soccer. Soccer players wear special clothes.

shirt

shorts

socks

soccer ball

shin guards

cleats

Teams must practice. It's fun!

A team gets the ball in the other team's goal. One point!

Teams show they are good sports. "Good game!" they say.

Connections

Comparing Texts

R2.2
R3.3
LS1.5

1. What did you learn about soccer from the story? What more did you learn from the article?

2. What games and sports have you played at school or at home?

3. What is your favorite game or sport? Why?

Writing

W2.1

Draw a picture of yourself learning to play a game or sport. Write what happened. Write some of the words you said.

I learned to play Tee Ball.
I had to practice a lot.
Now I can hit the ball.
It's fun!

Run!

I hit it!

Phonics

Make and read new words.

Start with **<u>long</u>**.

Change **l** to **s**.

Add **t** **r** after **s**.

Change **o** to **i**.

Take out **r**.

Fluency Practice

Read with a partner. Take turns reading pages of the story. Make it sound as if the characters are really talking. Remember to pause a little at commas and end marks.

Reading 2.2 Respond to *who, what, when, where,* and *how* questions; Reading 3.3 Recollect, talk, and write about books read during the school year; Writing 2.1 Write brief narratives (e.g., fictional, autobiographical) describing an experience; Listening and Speaking 1.5 Use descriptive words when speaking about people, places, things, and events.

Contents

Lesson 11

1 **Decodable Story**

Sid Scores

by Deanne W. Kells   illustrated by Pierre Pratt

2 **Genre: Nonfiction**

Land of Ice

by Norbert Wu

My Father's Feet

by Judy Sierra

3 **Genre: Poetry**

Phonics

Words with <u>or</u> and <u>ore</u>

Words to Know

Review

lives

was

now

Sid Scores

by Deanne W. Kells

illustrated by Pierre Pratt

Sid lives in the North.
He likes all sports.

Sid was born to win.
Sid scores and scores.
Win, Sid, win!

Sid can swim more than six laps.
He has good form.

Sid can do more.
He can jump past the cord.

Sid can flip and flop.
He can skim and skid.
More, Sid, more!

Sid is sore and worn out.
He will rest now.

Sid will snort and snore.

Sid will score more in the morning.

Phonics Skill

Words with or and ore

R1.10
R1.12

The letters **or** and **ore** can stand for the sound at the beginning of **orange**, in the middle of **fork**, and at the end of **store**.

orange

fork

store

CALIFORNIA STANDARDS
ENGLISH-LANGUAGE ARTS STANDARDS—Reading 1.10 Generate the sounds from all the letters and letter patterns, including consonant blends and long- and short-vowel patterns (i.e., phonograms), and blend those sounds into recognizable words; **Reading 1.12** Use knowledge of vowel digraphs and r-controlled letter-sound associations to read words.

**Look at each picture. Read the words.
Which word tells about the picture?**

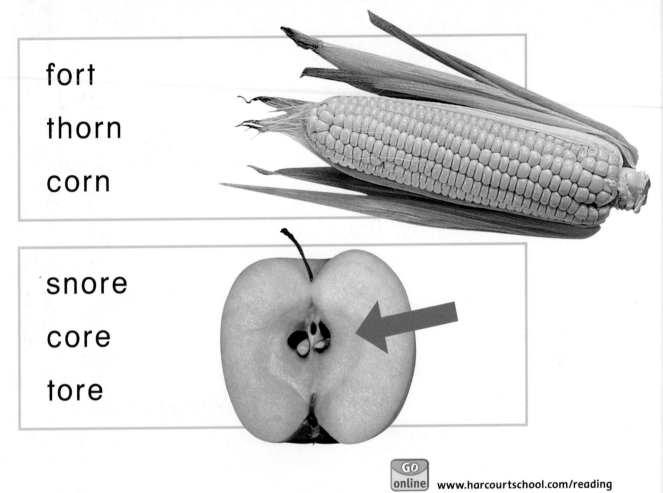

fort

thorn

corn

snore

core

tore

GO online www.harcourtschool.com/reading

Try This!

Read the sentences.

We went to the store for food.
My mom got some corn. My
dad got more eggs. I got a
new hat and wore it home.

Words to Know

High-Frequency Words

R1.11

very

cold

fish

their

from

animals

under

CALIFORNIA STANDARDS
ENGLISH-LANGUAGE ARTS STANDARDS—Reading 1.11 Read common, irregular sight words (e.g., *the, have, said, come, give, of*).

It is **very cold**. Many **fish** live here. Fish use **their** fins to swim. What does this fish eat? Big fish can eat small fish or get food **from** plants.

More **animals** live here. Many of them can swim **under** the water, too.

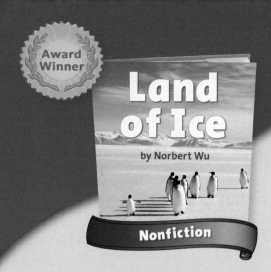

Land of Ice
by Norbert Wu

Nonfiction

R2.1

Genre Study
A **nonfiction** selection gives many facts about real things and often has photographs.

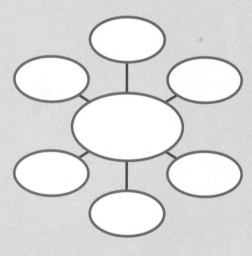

R2.6

Comprehension Strategy
Monitor Comprehension: Make Inferences Think about what the words say and what you already know to figure out what the selection is about.

 CALIFORNIA STANDARDS
ENGLISH-LANGUAGE ARTS STANDARDS—
Reading 2.1 Identify text that uses sequence or other logical order; **Reading 2.6** Relate prior knowledge to textual information.

Land of Ice

by Norbert Wu

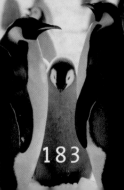

This is a land of ice.
It is very cold.

What is out here?
Can things live in
this land?

Look! This is a seal with a
small pup that was just born.
How can seals live here?

Seals have lots of fat and thick fur. This makes them snug.

Here is a small penguin.

This sort of penguin makes
nests on rocks and cliffs.
Penguins come from eggs.

Do more things live here?
Let's go under the ice.

It's beautiful! You can still see the sun.

You can see red sea stars.

There are animals that look like plants!

You can see an
octopus, too.

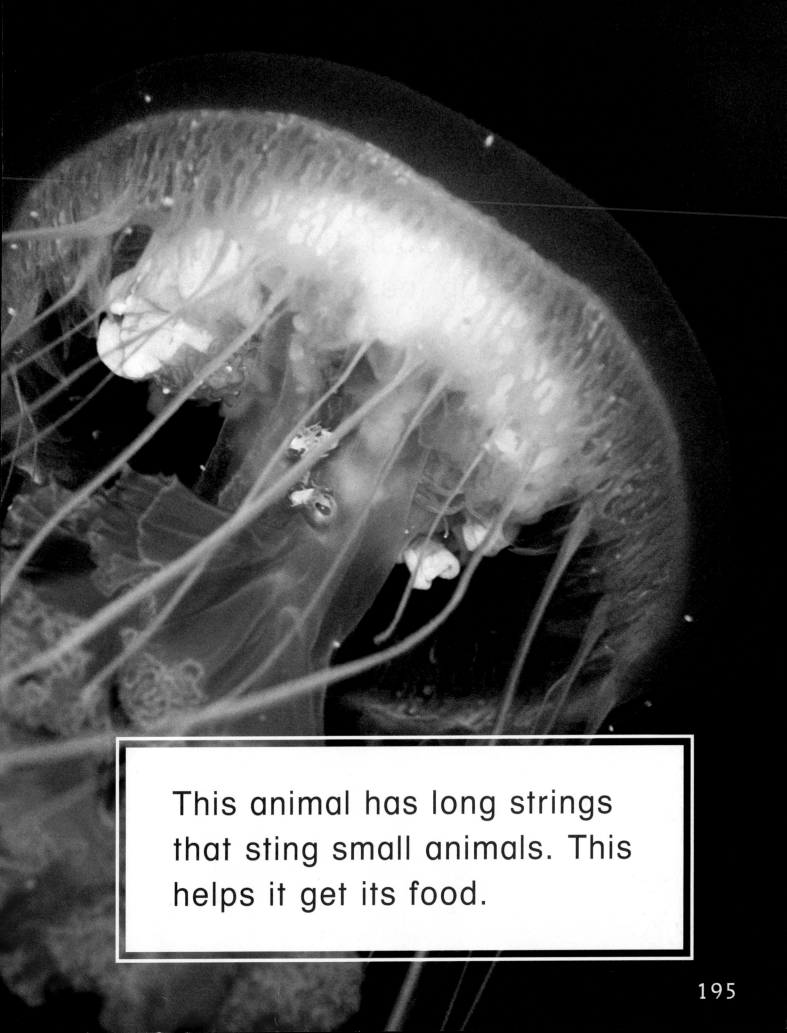

This animal has long strings that sting small animals. This helps it get its food.

This small fish likes ice. It does not get too cold. It has a nest of eggs in the ice.

This mom is helping her little one swim in the cold water.

Here are some more penguins.
Look at them go!

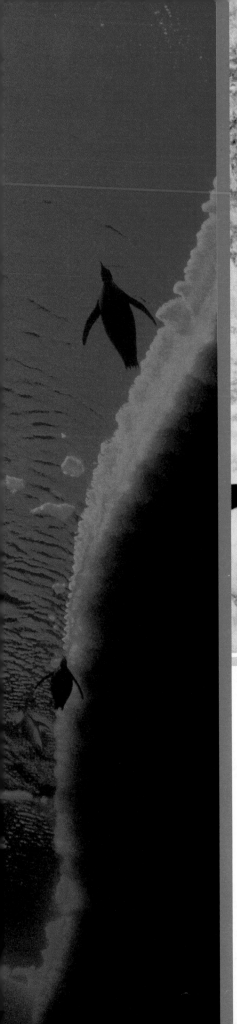

They use their wings to swim very fast. Flap, flap, flap! Where will they go next?

This IS a land of ice...
and much more!

Think Critically

R2.2
R2.6
R2.7
W2.2

1 How is the land different from what is under the water? How is it the same? COMPARE AND CONTRAST

2 What are some animals that live in the land of ice? DETAILS

3 Why do you think penguins like to live there? DRAW CONCLUSIONS

4 Does it look as if people could live there? Why or why not? MAKE INFERENCES

5 **WRITE** Write about the most interesting animal in "Land of Ice."

WRITING RESPONSE

CALIFORNIA STANDARDS
ENGLISH-LANGUAGE ARTS STANDARDS—Reading 2.2 Respond to *who, what, when, where,* and *how* questions; **Reading 2.6** Relate prior knowledge to textual information; **Reading 2.7** Retell the central ideas of simple expository or narrative passages; **Writing 2.2** Write brief expository descriptions of a real object, person, place, or event, using sensory details.

Meet the Author/Photographer
Norbert Wu

Norbert Wu likes to take pictures in unusual places, like under the ice in Antarctica! He has seen many animals there, including lots of penguins. He says that penguins walk oddly on land, but are at home in the water. They swim around fast, just like little jet planes!

"I wrote this story because I want you to know that our world is a beautiful and fragile place."

GO online www.harcourtschool.com/reading

203

My
Father's
Feet

by Judy Sierra

Poetry

My Father's Feet

by Judy Sierra

To keep myself up off the ice,
I find my father's feet are nice.
I snuggle in his belly fluff,
And that's how I stay warm enough.

But when my father takes a walk,
My cozy world begins to rock.
He shuffles left, I hold on tight.
Oh no! He's wobbling to the right.

Not left again! Oops, here he goes.
Do you suppose my father knows
I'm hanging on to his warm toes?

Contents

Lesson 12

1 Decodable Story

Fox and His Big Wish

by Sandra Widener
Illustrated by Will Terry

2 Genre: Myth

King Midas and His Gold

by Patricia and Fredrick McKissack

illustrated by Josée Masse

3 Gold and Money

Genre: Nonfiction

Fox and His Big Wish

by Sandra Widener
illustrated by Will Terry

Fox wanted a snack.
He wished for a big, fresh fish.

Ping!
Fox got his wish!

The fish was big.
It was too big for a snack.

Fox's fish was too big for his dish.
It was too big for his mat.

His fish was not a fresh fish now.
It smelled bad!

Fox did not like his big fish.
He wished that fish was small.

Fox did not get his wish.
That fish went in the trash!

Focus Skill

 Setting

The **setting** is when and where the story takes place.

Look at the picture.

The setting is a city at night.

CALIFORNIA STANDARDS
ENGLISH-LANGUAGE ARTS STANDARDS—Reading 3.1 Identify and describe the elements of plot, setting, and character(s) in a story, as well as the story's beginning, middle, and ending.

Tell about this picture. What is the setting? How can you tell?

Try This!

Look at the picture. Choose the words that name the setting.

- a day at the zoo

- an evening at the beach

- a day at the park

 www.harcourtschool.com/reading

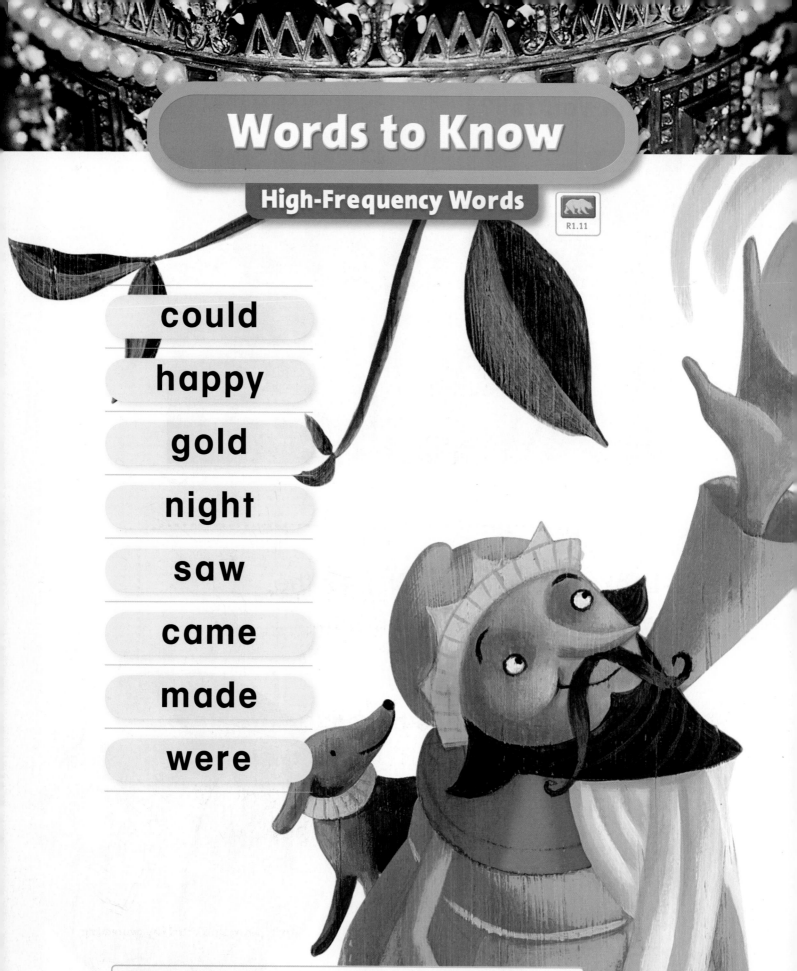

Words to Know

High-Frequency Words

R1.11

could

happy

gold

night

saw

came

made

were

CALIFORNIA STANDARDS
ENGLISH-LANGUAGE ARTS STANDARDS—Reading 1.11 Read common, irregular sight words (e.g., *the, have, said, come, give, of*).

The king asked, "What **could** make me **happy**? Will this **gold** apple make me happy?"

That **night**, the king **saw** a dog. The dog **came** up to him. It licked the king's hand. This **made** the king grin. From then on, they **were** very happy!

 www.harcourtschool.com/reading

221

by Patricia and
Fredrick McKissack

illustrated
by Josée Masse

Myth

Genre Study

A **myth** is an old story that teaches a lesson. It has make-believe characters and events.

Characters	Setting

↓ Beginning ↓

Beginning

↓

Middle

↓

Ending

Comprehension Strategy

Ask Questions As you read, ask yourself questions and look for the answers. Where does King Midas get gold?

CALIFORNIA STANDARDS
ENGLISH-LANGUAGE ARTS STANDARDS—
Reading 3.1 Identify and describe the elements of plot, setting, and character(s) in a story, as well as the story's beginning, middle, and ending.

King Midas
and
His Gold

**by Patricia and
Fredrick McKissack**

illustrated by Josée Masse

Midas was king, but he wasn't happy.
"I wish for gold," he said. "That will
make me happy."

Ping!
The king got his wish.

King Midas picked a fresh apple.
Ping!
In a flash, it was gold.

Ping! Ping! Ping! Ping!
His cup, dish, box, and shelf
were gold.

King Midas felt happy. He had
more and more gold!

King Midas saw a red flower.
Ping! It was gold. King Midas
did not like that.

The king's dog rushed up to him.

Ping! His dog was gold. King Midas did not like that at all.

King Midas was king, but
he was not very happy. He
could not eat a thing.

Ping! Ping!
King Midas could not rest at night.
His blanket and his bed were gold.

Ping! His pet cat was gold.
Ping! The queen was gold.

"Get back!" cried the king.
"GET BACK!"

Ping!
The princess was gold.
The king was shocked!

All he had was gold and more gold!
King Midas felt very sad.
"I wish for no more gold," he said.
He got his wish.

Ping!
Back came the princess, the queen,
his cat, his dog, the flower, the
apple, and all of his things!

King Midas could eat and rest.

"No more gold," he said, and
this made him happy.

Think Critically

R2.2
R2.7
R3.1
W2.1

1 How can you tell that this story takes place long ago? SETTING

2 What happens to the apple when the king touches it? DETAILS

3 Why doesn't the king like it when his dog turns to gold? MAKE INFERENCES

4 Why is King Midas glad to lose his golden touch? DRAW CONCLUSIONS

5 **WRITE** Write about something you wish for and tell why. WRITING RESPONSE

CALIFORNIA STANDARDS
ENGLISH-LANGUAGE ARTS STANDARDS—Reading 2.2 Respond to *who, what, when, where,* and *how* questions; **Reading 2.7** Retell the central ideas of simple expository or narrative passages; **Reading 3.1** Identify and describe the elements of plot, setting, and character(s) in a story, as well as the story's beginning, middle, and ending; **Writing 2.1** Write brief narratives (e.g., fictional, autobiographical) describing an experience.

Meet the Authors

Patricia and Fredrick McKissack

Patricia and Fredrick McKissack met when they were teenagers. Before they began writing books together, Fredrick owned a construction company. Patricia was a teacher. They especially like to write books that show how a person solves a problem.

Meet the Illustrator
Josée Masse

Josée Masse started drawing when she was very young. Her father was a painter. As a child, she would draw with him in his studio.

Josée Masse has pets—a dog, a cat, many fish, and things her daughter brings from outside, like bugs!

 www.harcourtschool.com/reading

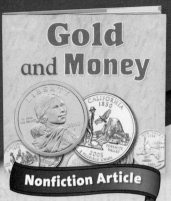

Gold and Money

Nonfiction Article

Teacher Read-Aloud

Gold and Money

The United States has a golden coin.
It is worth one dollar.

front

back

It shows Sacajawea. Long ago,
she helped explorers find
their way across America.

Each state has a special quarter.
The pictures show things that are
important to that state.

California Quarter

front   **back**

Connections

Comparing Texts

1 Do you think King Midas would want the coins from "Gold and Money"? Why or why not?

2 What do you think makes people happy?

3 Tell about a place that makes you happy. Why are you happy there?

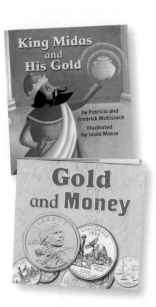

Writing
W1.1

Write Happy on one side of a chart and Sad on the other. List the things that you think make King Midas happy and sad.

Happy	Sad
drink	gold food
rest	gold dog
family	gold bed

CALIFORNIA STANDARDS
ENGLISH-LANGUAGE ARTS STANDARDS—Reading 1.10 Generate the sounds from all the letters and letter patterns, including consonant blends and long- and short-vowel patterns (i.e., phonograms), and blend those sounds into recognizable words; **Reading 1.16** Read aloud with fluency in a manner that sounds like natural speech; *(continued)*

Phonics
R1.10

Make and read new words.

Start with **hut**.

Add **s** in front of **h**.

Change **s** **h** to **r**.

Change **t** to **s** **h**.

Change **r** to **w** and **u** to **i**.

Fluency Practice
R1.16

Read the story aloud with classmates. Look for exclamation points. Use your voice to show excitement and other strong feelings.

Ping! The king got his wish.

Reading 2.2 Respond to *who, what, when, where,* and *how* questions; **Reading 3.3** Recollect, talk, and write about books read during the school year; **Writing 1.1** Select a focus when writing; **Listening and Speaking 1.5** Use descriptive words when speaking about people, places, things, and events.

Glossary

What Is a Glossary?

A glossary can help you read a word. You can look up the word and read it in a sentence. Each word has a picture to help you.

gift   **Jill got a gift.**

animals   The **animals** have fur.

arms   She is holding out her **arms.**

C

cold   My hands are **cold!**

D

day   We run all **day.**

E

eat   This snack is good to **eat.**

feet   Here are my **feet.**

fish   The **fish** is in the water.

food   Look at all the **food!**

line   I made a **line** with string.

new   She got something **new.**

night   He went to bed last **night.**

school   This is my **school.**

time   What **time** is it?

U

under   She is **under** it.

W

water   We splash in the **water.**

Decodable Stories Word Lists

The following words appear in the Decodable Stories in Book 1-2.

Lesson 7   "Ten Eggs"

Word Count: 50

High-Frequency Words	Decodable Words*	
make	a	**Jen**
the	and	**Ken**
what	**best**	**mess**
	big	mixed
	did	Mom
	eggs	pan
	get	**rest**
	got	six
	had	**ten**
	help	**went**
	hens	**yes**
	in	**yet**

*Words with /e/e appear in **boldface** type.

Lesson 10   "Frog Gets His Song"

Word Count: 94

High-Frequency Words	Decodable Words*	
are	a	I
be	and	in
do	asked	let
go	at	**long**
have	big	**lungs**
her	can't	**Ming**
looked	did	**Ming's**
me	**fangs**	**rang**
no	filled	**sang**
out	Frog	**sing**
said	frogs	**singing**
you	gets	snapped
	grin	**song**
	grip	still
	grunted	stop
	had	then
	help	will
	him	with
	his	yelled
	hissed	yes

*Words with /ng/*ng* appear in **boldface** type.

Lesson 11 "Sid Scores"

Word Count: 79

High-Frequency Words	Decodable Words*	
do	all	rest
good	and	**score**
he	**born**	**scores**
likes	can	Sid
lives	**cord**	six
now	flip	skid
out	flop	skim
the	**form**	**snore**
to	has	**snort**
	in	**sore**
	is	**sports**
	jump	swim
	laps	than
	more	was
	morning	will
	North	win
	past	**worn**

*Words with /ôr/ *or, ore* appear in **boldface** type.

Lesson 12 "Fox and His Big Wish"

Word Count: 83

High-Frequency Words	Decodable Words*	
he	a	in
like	and	it
now	bad	mat
the	big	not
too	did	ping
wanted	**dish**	small
was	**fish**	smelled
	for	snack
	Fox	that
	Fox's	**trash**
	fresh	went
	get	**wish**
	got	**wished**
	his	

*Words with /sh/sh appear in **boldface** type.

English-Language Arts Content Standards

 **READING**

1.0 **Word Analysis, Fluency, and Systematic Vocabulary Development**
Students understand the basic features of reading. They select letter patterns and know how to translate them into spoken language by using phonics, syllabication, and word parts. They apply this knowledge to achieve fluent oral and silent reading.

Concepts About Print

1.1 Match oral words to printed words.

1.2 Identify the title and author of a reading selection.

1.3 Identify letters, words, and sentences.

Phonemic Awareness

1.4 Distinguish initial, medial, and final sounds in single-syllable words.

1.5 Distinguish long- and short-vowel sounds in orally stated single-syllable words (e.g., *bit/bite*).

1.6 Create and state a series of rhyming words, including consonant blends.

1.7 Add, delete, or change target sounds to change words (e.g., change *cow* to *how*; *pan* to *an*).

1.8 Blend two to four phonemes into recognizable words (e.g., */c/a/t/* = cat; */f/l/a/t/* = flat).

1.9 Segment single-syllable words into their components (e.g., cat = /c/a/t/; splat = /s/p/l/a/t/; rich = /r/i/ch/).

Decoding and Word Recognition

1.10 Generate the sounds from all the letters and letter patterns, including consonant blends and long- and short-vowel patterns (i.e., phonograms), and blend those sounds into recognizable words.

1.11 Read common, irregular sight words (e.g., *the, have, said, come, give, of*).

1.12 Use knowledge of vowel digraphs and r-controlled letter-sound associations to read words.

1.13 Read compound words and contractions.

1.14 Read inflectional forms (e.g., *-s, -ed, -ing*) and root words (e.g., *look, looked, looking*).

1.15 Read common word families (e.g., *-ite, -ate*).

1.16 Read aloud with fluency in a manner that sounds like natural speech.

Vocabulary and Concept Development

1.17 Classify grade-appropriate categories of words (e.g., concrete collections of animals, foods, toys).

2.0 **Reading Comprehension**
Students read and understand grade-level-appropriate material. They draw upon a variety of comprehension strategies as needed (e.g., generating

and responding to essential questions, making predictions, comparing information from several sources.) The selections in *Recommended Literature, Kindergarten Through Grade Twelve* illustrate the quality and complexity of the materials to be read by students. In addition to their regular school reading, by grade four, students read one-half million words annually, including a good representation of grade-level-appropriate narrative and expository text (e.g., classic and contemporary literature, magazines, newpapers, online information). In grade one, students begin to make progress toward this goal.

Structural Features of Informational Materials

2.1   Identify text that uses sequence or other logical order.

Comprehension and Analysis of Grade-Level-Appropriate Text

2.2   Respond to *who, what, when, where,* and *how* questions.

2.3   Follow one-step written instructions.

2.4   Use context to resolve ambiguities about word and sentence meanings.

2.5   Confirm predictions about what will happen next in a text by identifying key words (i.e., signpost words).

2.6   Relate prior knowledge to textual information.

2.7   Retell the central ideas of simple expository or narrative passages.

3.0 Literary Response and Analysis

Students read and respond to a wide variety of significant works of children's literature. They distinguish between the structural features of the text and the literary terms or elements (e.g., theme, plot, setting, characters). The selections in *Recommended Literature, Kindergarten Through Grade Twelve* illustrate the quality and complexity of the materials to be read by students.

Narrative Analysis of Grade-Level-Appropriate Text

3.1 Identify and describe the elements of plot, setting, and character(s) in a story, as well as the story's beginning, middle, and ending.

3.2 Describe the roles of authors and illustrators and their contributions to print materials.

3.3 Recollect, talk, and write about books read during the school year.

 WRITING

1.0 Writing Strategies

Students write clear and coherent sentences and paragraphs that develop a central idea. Their writing shows they consider the audience and purpose. Students progress through the stages of the writing process (e.g., prewriting, drafting, revising, editing successive versions).

Organization and Focus

1.1 Select a focus when writing.

1.2 Use descriptive words when writing.

Penmanship

1.3 Print legibly and space letters, words, and sentences appropriately.

2.0 Writing Applications (Genres and Their Characteristics)

Students write compositions that describe and explain familiar objects, events, and experiences. Student writing demonstrates a command of standard American English and the drafting, research, and organizational strategies outlined in Writing Standard 1.0.

Using the writing strategies of grade one outlined in Writing Standard 1.0, students:

2.1 Write brief narratives (e.g., fictional, autobiographical) describing an experience.

2.2 Write brief expository descriptions of a real object, person, place, or event, using sensory details.

WRITTEN AND ORAL ENGLISH LANGUAGE CONVENTIONS

The standards for written and oral English language conventions have been placed between those for writing and for listening and speaking because these conventions are essential to both sets of skills.

1.0 Written and Oral English Language Conventions

Students write and speak with a command of standard English conventions appropriate to this grade level.

Sentence Structure

1.1 Write and speak in complete, coherent sentences.

Grammar

1.2 Identify and correctly use singular and plural nouns.

1.3 Identify and correctly use contractions (e.g., *isn't, aren't, can't, won't*) and singular possessive pronouns (e.g., *my/mine, his/her, hers, your/s*) in writing and speaking.

Punctuation

1.4 Distinguish between declarative, exclamatory, and interrogative sentences.

1.5 Use a period, exclamation point, or question mark at the end of sentences.

1.6 Use knowledge of the basic rules of punctuation and capitalization when writing.

Capitalization

1.7 Capitalize the first word of a sentence, names of people, and the pronoun *I*.

Spelling

1.8 Spell three- and four-letter short-vowel words and grade-level-appropriate sight words correctly.

1.0 Listening and Speaking Strategies

Students listen critically and respond appropriately to oral communication. They speak in a manner that guides the listener to understand important ideas by using proper phrasing, pitch, and modulation.

Comprehension

1.1 Listen attentively.

1.2 Ask questions for clarification and understanding.

1.3 Give, restate, and follow simple two-step directions.

Organization and Delivery of Oral Communication

1.4 Stay on the topic when speaking.

1.5 Use descriptive words when speaking about people, places, things, and events.

2.0 Speaking Applications (Genres and Their Characteristics)

Students deliver brief recitations and oral presentations about familiar experiences or interests that are organized around a coherent thesis statement. Student speaking demonstrates a command of standard American English and the organizational and delivery strategies outlined in Listening and Speaking Standard 1.0.

Using the speaking strategies of grade one outlined in Listening and Speaking Standard 1.0, students:

2.1 Recite poems, rhymes, songs, and stories.

2.2 Retell stories using basic story grammar and relating the sequence of story events by answering *who, what, when, where, why,* and *how* questions.

2.3 Relate an important life event or personal experience in a simple sequence.

2.4 Provide descriptions with careful attention to sensory detail.

Acknowledgments

For permission to reprint copyrighted material, grateful acknowledgment is made to the following sources:

English-Language Arts Content Standards for California Public Schools reproduced by permission, California Department of Education, CDE Press, 1430 N. Street, Suite 3207, Sacramento, CA 95814.

Curtis Brown, Ltd.: From *King Midas and His Gold* by Patricia & Fredrick McKissack. Text copyright © 1986 by Patricia & Fredrick McKissack. Published by Children's Press.
Harcourt, Inc.: "My Father's Feet" from *Antarctic Antics: A Book of Penguin Poems* by Judy Sierra. Text copyright © 1998 by Judy Sierra.
Lee & Low Books Inc.: "Cornfield Leaves" from *Children of Long Ago* by Lessie Jones Little. Text copyright © 2000 by Weston W. Little, Sr. Estate; text copyright © 1998 by Weston Little.

Photo Credits

Placement Key: (t) top; (b) bottom; (r) right; (l) left; (c) center; (bg) background; (fg) foreground; (i) inset.

5 (t) The Grand Design/SuperStock; 6 (t) The Grand Design/SuperStock; 7 (br) The Grand Design/SuperStock; 8 (inset) Digital Stock/Corbis; 12 (c) The Grand Design/SuperStock; 15 (b) Burke/Triolo Productions/FoodPix/PictureQuest; 24 (cr) Corbis; 24 (bl) Raymond Kasprzak; RF/Shutterstock; 24 (br) RubberBall Productions/Getty Images/Harcourt Index; 25 (t) Benelux/Zefa/Corbis; 44 (tl) Steve Yeater / Black Star; 45 (tr) Steve Yeater / Black Star; 46 (b) Makoto Fujio/Dex Image/PictureQuest; 53 (b) C Squared Studios/Getty images; 62 (c) Laszlo Selly/Food Pix/Jupiterimages; 87 (br) Michael Garland; 88 (bc) Frasnk Cezus/Getty Images; 88 (tr) Getty Images; 88 (br) Steve Satushek/Getty Images; 89 (l) Masterfile Royalty Free; 89 (r) Primsa /Superstock; 90 (t) Yuriy Korchagin; RF/Shutterstock; 93 (bl) Food Collection/Getty Images; 102 (t) Anette Linnea Rasmussen; RF/Shutterstock; 102 (c) Jakez; RF/Shutterstock; 104 (t) Leonid Nishko; RF/Shutterstock; 104 (b) photocuisine/Corbis; 107 (c) Royalty-Free/Corbis; 109 (c) Daniel Attia/zefa/Corbis; 110 (c) B. Runks/S. Schoenberger/Grant Heilman Photography; 111 (tl) Gerard Mathieu/Getty Images; 111 (tr) Mark Moffett/Minden Pictures; 112 (c) Jim Brandenburg/Minden Pictures; 113 (tl) Gerry Ellis/Minden Pictures; 113 (tr) Inga Spence / Getty Images; 114 (t) Tim Laman / getty images; 115 (c) BLOOMimage/Getty Images; 116 (t) Roy Morsch/ Corbis; 117 (c) Nigel Cattlin/Photo Researchers, Inc.; 118 (c) Sylvain Grandadam/Getty Images; 118 (t) Theo Allofs/Photonica/Getty Images; 119 (br) John Foxx/Getty Images; 119 (bl) Marion Brenner/Picture Quest; 120 (c) Scott Camazine/Photo Researchers, Inc.; 121 (t) B. Runk/S. Schoenberger/Grant Heilman Photography; 121 (inset) Gerry Ellis/ Getty images; 122 (t) Dennis Gottlieb/PictureQuest; 123 (c) age fotostock/SuperStock; 124 (t) Theo Allofs / Getty Images; 125 (c) Ariel Sjelley/Corbis; 126 (bg) Bill Ross/Corbis; 130 (t) Nicholas Piccillo/Shutterstock; 133 (br) Photo Disc Inc.; 143 (br) Tom Rosenthal/SuperStock; 144 (t) JD; RF/Shutterstock; 162 (l) Mike Falco / Black Star; 163 (r) Mike Falco / Black Star; 164 (inset) Wide Group/Getty Images; 165 (cl) Amdrew Olney/Getty Images; 165 (tl) Charles Gupton/Corbis; 165 (bg) Estelle Klawitter/zefa/ Corbis; 165 (bl) Lynn Siler Photography/Alamy; 166 (t) Ariel Skelley/Corbis; 169 (b) age fotostock/SuperStock; 178 (t) Silense; RF/Shutterstock; 180 (t) Corbis; 181 - 201 © 2005 Norbert Wu, www.norbertwu.com; 202 (bg) Dale Stokes/www.norbertwu.com; 204 (c) Frans Lanting/Minden Pictures; 205 (tr) Frans Lanting/Minden Pictures; 206 (t) Giangrande Alessia/Shutterstock; 209 (bl) Brand X/SuperStock; 218 (c) Stanislav Khrapov; RF/Shutterstock; 219 (t) Stuart McCall/Photographer's Choice; 242 (b) Bob Ransom / Black Star; 243 (cl) Rene' De Carufel / Balck Star; 245 (cl) Quarter coin image from the United States Mint; 245 United States coin image from the United States Mint; 245 United States coin image from the United States Mint; 245 United States coin image from the United States Mint; 245 (cr) United States coin image from the United States Mint; 245 United States coin image from the United States Mint; 245 United States coin image from the United States Mint; 254 (c) George Doyle/Stockbyte Platinum/Getty Images; 255 (t) Thomas Barwick/Photodisc Red/Getty Images.
All other photos © Houghton Mifflin Harcourt Publishers.

Illustration Credits

Cover Art; Laura and Eric Ovresat, Artlab, Inc.